The

Masterpreneur Playbook

2nd Edition

To Amber,

I hope you find this to be a valuable resource for growing your

hot sauce baron

Sally

The
Masterpreneur Playbook

2nd Edition

ANDREW FRAZIER, MBA, CFA

SMALL BUSINESS PRO UNIVERSITY PRESS
MONTCLAIR, NEW JERSEY

"This is a true common sense guide. It tells you how to run your enterprise like a business, not a pastime or hobby. For those who need direction on the important basics for success, this is the book for you."

John J. Webb
President
Tri-South Cigna

Of all the people I have collaborated with; Andrew Frazier is the real deal. He fundamentally understands the challenges small businesses face and can quickly develop real world solutions that drive impressive results, which I have seen firsthand.

Gene Bohensky
President, The Alternative Board Northern New Jersey
Certified Business Coach, Archer Strategies

Andrew and "Small Business Like A Pro" are much needed voices and champions of the country's largest employers – small business collectively. The book is a practical must-read and belongs in the library of anyone who owns a small business and especially those who aspire to the enterprise ranks and "to be able to have their business function independently of the owner." The book is also a valuable resource for coaches and consultants who want an easy to understand reference they can use to help increase the operational competence of their small business clients.

David Greene
President, Urbanomics Consulting Group

This book is available at special discounts for bulk purchases, sales promotions, premiums, fundraising, or educational use.

For details, e-mail: info@SmallBusinessLikeAPro.com

Small Business Pro University Press
email: info@SmallBusinessLikeAPro.com
Website: www.SBProU.com/sbprou-press

Cover Design and Layout: Andrew Frazier Jr.
Diagram Illustrator: Steven Robinson
Editors: Barry Cohen and John Larrier

Library of Congress Control Number: NRC112040

ISBN 978-1-970129-05-2

Printed in the United States of America

Table of Contents

Foreword

Today's business environment has provided some of the most unique challenges in our lifetimes. Not since the Great Depression of 1929 and the Great Recession of 2009, have we seen such a set of circumstances impacting our business community. Small, minority, women, veteran, and family-owned businesses have been especially hard hit by the effects of the COVID-19 economy.

But it is by no means all gloom and doom. In every cloud, there is a silver lining. Such times as these present not only challenges, but also opportunities. Consider that some of America's—in fact, the world's greatest companies were started during recessions. To wit, General Electric and Microsoft are just two examples. Many individuals enter entrepreneurship out of necessity during tight job markets.

So, how do we advance our knowledge when we are practically consumed with the activities surrounding starting, operating, and attempting to grow our businesses every day? That is where this book comes in. We must first understand the landscape we are trying to traverse and what path our journey will take. The Masterpreneur™ Playbook does just that. This book lays out the steps you must take once you identify where you are on the journey, in order to progress toward the ultimate phase—scaling your business.

During my time as Executive Director of the Rothman Institute I was pleased to partner with Andrew Frazier, the architect of this wonderful program. He was a top consultant to smaller businesses and provided valuable knowledge. He was one of our guest experts at the Rothman Institute's events. For those who are not yet familiar with the Rothman Institute of Innovation and Entrepreneurship, it is under the umbrella of the Silberman College of Business at Fairleigh Dickinson University. The Rothman Institute has been advising area businesses for many years. We were proud to partner with the Small Business Pro University to offer certification programs designed to help small business owners advance their knowledge and achieve greater success.

Once you have read and absorbed the content of the Masterpreneur™ Playbook I encourage you to take the next step and sign up for one of his Masterpreneur Training Programs.

Dr. Dale Caldwell
President
Centenary University

https://www.centenaryuniversity.edu/

Preface

The Masterpreneur Playbook shares valuable insights gained from coaching and consulting small business owners, as well as my education, business leadership roles, and entrepreneurial endeavors. It is a compilation of key learning and important perspectives gained from my diverse experiences with many different organizations.

As a business coach and consultant who has worked with 1,000+ business owners, I noticed several common patterns and themes:

- Your business can progress no further than you are prepared to take it.
- You must continually learn and develop your leadership skills if you want your company to grow and thrive.
- Achieving your goals and overcoming your challenges leads to new challenges to overcome and new goals to achieve.
- There are clear consistent patterns in the types of challenges that you will face and goals that you must achieve to grow.
- You must evolve and take on different roles and responsibilities throughout the process, some easier than others.
- You must create more and more structure as your business grows so you must develop your team and delegate more.
- You will need to obtain the necessary support and guidance since it is extremely difficult to transition through each stage.

The Masterpreneur Playbook is the next step in the evolution of my path to help entrepreneurs and small business owners successfully navigate the numerous challenges they face. It is a 5-Step Growth Plan for guiding them from start up to scaling. This book will help you understand the path to create the level of business success that you desire.

I'm glad that you chose this book as a resource, and I appreciate the opportunity to participate in your entrepreneurial journey. I look forward to guiding you along the path and it is my honor to provide you with some of the encouragement, education, and expertise needed to achieve your business goals. Let's get started.

Sincerely.

Andrew Frazier, MBA, CFA

Business Pro @ Small Business Like A Pro

Founder, Small Business Pro University (www.SBProU.com)

Introduction

Your decision to read The Masterpreneur™ Playbook is an indication of your commitment to your own success. I am confident that you will find it to be a valuable investment.

According to Oberlo.com, in 2019, 3.48 million applications to start a business in the U.S. were submitted. Unfortunately, nearly 50% of new businesses fail within the first five years. Businessweek.com reported: only about 40% of U.S. family-owned businesses turn into second-generation businesses, approximately 13% are passed down successfully to a third generation, and 3% to a fourth or beyond. Sobering statistics? Perhaps, but do not let the statistics deter you. Businesses with a solid, well thought out plan, the right talent and a commitment to a growth mindset do succeed. We have analyzed the success factors and codified them into the Masterpreneur Playbook™.

I developed The Masterpreneur Playbook™ for you. It is a proprietary 5-step Business Growth Plan for going from Starting-Up to Scaling your business. It meets business owners wherever they are in their business journey and helps guide them to create a sustainable enterprise that can successfully run without them.

Owning a business can be particularly challenging because there are so many things you need to know and do. However, it can also be extremely fulfilling and rewarding both personally and professionally. As an experienced business coach and consultant who has worked 1-on-1 with over 500 businesses, I have seen the good, the bad, and the ugly. Having owned several businesses myself, I learned firsthand, many of the pitfalls that are out there and figured out what it takes to run a successful business.

It took me 5 years to write my first book *Running Your Small Business Like A Pro: The More You Know, The Faster You Grow,* a guide to help business owners understand, navigate, and overcome many of the key challenges. *The Masterpreneur Playbook*™ builds upon those insights to focus specifically on the path that your business must travel and how you must evolve as a business owner.

"A Proven Plan"

The Masterpreneur Playbook™ lays out a proven plan for successfully taking your business from start-up to scaling by meeting you where you are and helping you identify how best to move forward. This is a proprietary methodology that was developed based on many years of experience, education, training, and mentorship. I learned about how critical the relationships you develop and maintain are to your success in business and in life. I understand why experience is more important than education but, the combination of both knowledge and wisdom is the key. I have experienced how owning a business can be painful, stressful, and lonely at times even when things are going well.

All business owners face challenges

Like many business owners you may be facing challenges. Do you own your business, or does your business own you.? Are you having cashflow issues, or do you need financing? Is your business growing? And are you making enough money? Can you take time off?

Do you Have a Tried-and-Tested Playbook for Moving Your Business Forward?

The best sports teams have a proven playbook, and every business should have one. Now you do! Most business owners have knowledge gaps to fill because there is so much that they need to know to run a successful business. Oftentimes, you do not know what you need to know, where to find the information, or the right path needed to grow.

It's easy to get confused or stuck. Too many business owners work long and hard hours for less money than working a job because they are on the wrong path. Break the cycle of low or no business growth with *The Masterpreneur Playbook*™ and go from Working IN Your Business to Working ON Your Business.

The Masterpreneur Journey

The *Masterpreneur Playbook*™ is a proven 5-Step Business Growth Plan for the journey you will take going from Starting-Up to Scaling your business. The Masterpreneur Path™ clearly and concisely outlines the way your organization needs to move forward by pointing out the challenges you will face and the goals you must achieve. "There is a difference between walking the path and knowing the path." Words of wisdom that Morpheus said to Neo in *The Matrix* Movie. Walking the path is about your personal leadership journey facing different trials and tribulations and learning from them. I call that the Masterpreneur Evolution™, a process of developing key leadership skills; and creating the organizational structure necessary for taking each step and reaching the ultimate goal.

Why is Achieving the Ultimate Goal So Important?

There are three primary reasons for creating a sustainable enterprise that can run successfully without you:

1.   You will make more money faster and easier

2.   You will be able to focus more effort on growing your business and have more time to enjoy with your family

3.   You will have a more valuable business with succession/exit planning options

That is a goal that most every business owner envisions, but very few ever achieve. My *Masterpreneur Playbook*™ lays out a proven plan for successfully taking your business from start-up to scaling by meeting you where you are and helping you identify how best to move forward. I created the Small Business Pro University www.SBProU.com to provide you with the knowledge, resources, tools, guidance, and support that you will need to successfully implement *The Masterpreneur Playbook*™.

The Masterpreneur Path

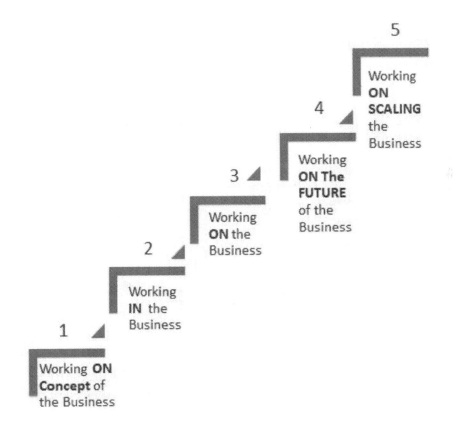

The Masterpreneur Path™ outlines how you and your organization need to move forward by identifying the challenges you will face and the goals that you must achieve. It is also a way to measure where you are along the journey, to meet you where you are, and serve as a guide, pointing you in the right direction to achieve your desired goals. The order of these 5-Steps is crucial because you must crawl before you can walk, walk before you can run, and run before you can fly.

"Failing to Plan is Planning to Fail"

Your business must go through these 5-Steps to become a sustainable enterprise that can run successfully without you:

1. **Working ON the Concept of Your Business** – identifying the problem you're seeking to solve, the product/service related solution you'll provide, who your customers will be, and how you'll get them to buy from you.

2. **Working IN Your Business** – focused on the day-to-day product/service delivery and sales activities.

3. **Working ON Your Business** – focused on continually improving business operations and profitability.

4. **Working ON the Future of Your Business** – focused on planning and preparing to scale your business.

5. **Working ON Scaling Your Business** – leading implementation of strategic plan to significantly increase revenue and profitability.

Which step are you on? _____

- Are you working on the concept of your business? Is most of your time spent developing your plans and launching the business?
- Are you working in your business? Are you spending most of your time focused on the day-to-day or week-to-week product/service delivery? Do you need to have a good supervisor or lead employee to free you up to work on the business?

- Are you working on your business? Do you spend most of your time focused on analyzing your business for opportunities to continually improve and optimize processes, procedures, and systems?
- Are you working on the future of your business? Do you spend much of your time doing research and strategic planning for growth? Are you developing key relationships that can be helpful in scaling your business?

Key Challenges

There are many challenges you will face during your business journey. However, there is one key challenge that you must overcome at each step along the Masterpreneur Path™ to move forward. Unfortunately, many business owners get stuck because they focus on the wrong challenges at the wrong times. They either do not know the critical challenge that they face, or they do not understand how to overcome it. *The Masterpreneur Playbook*™ provides the answers you need to identify and solve the key challenges that you will face in each step of growing your business.

Solving Problems Is Key

Let's take a quick look at the key challenges you will have to overcome at each step in the Masterpreneur Path™.

1) **Developing A Marketing Plan** – your marketing plan needs to outline the business opportunity (research), your unique value proposition (products/services), and how you plan to reach/convert potential customers (strategy).

2) **Finding the Right Target Market** – your target market should be the most likely people to purchase your products and services, which is usually different from the one outlined in your original business plan. As a result, you must gather and evaluate feedback from the marketplace to continually refine, define, and test your products/services, offerings, and messaging until sales are consistently increasing.

3) **Managing Effectively** – once you have consistent revenue, it's time to optimize your business to maximize profitability and scalability. This requires you to analyze your business model, set appropriate goals, and measure performance. It also involves setting policies, creating procedures, and developing systems.

4) **Developing A Leadership Team** – it starts with preparing yourself to effectively hire, onboard, and lead managers within your organization. You must overcome the temptation to micromanage so that you can focus on higher level tasks for growing your business that are important, but not urgent.

5) **Managing Cash Flow** – a business requires cash to fuel its growth. Many businesses fail because they grow too fast and run out of money. You must actively manage expected cash inflows and outflows to ensure there is always enough liquidity available.

Which of these challenges are you facing? _____

- Have you done appropriate market research and developed an initial marketing plan?
- Is your product accepted in the marketplace and selling at a profitable level?
- How effective is your marketing and how efficient are your operations?
- Do you have a management team where each member knows more than you about their area of responsibility?
- Have you accessed the capital necessary to achieve your growth goals?

What other challenges are you facing? _____

- Cash Flow?
- Sales?
- Financing?
- Staffing?
- Productivity
- Others?

Business Goals

There are also specific business goals associated with each step on the Masterpreneur Path™. Accomplishing these goals is the foundation of moving your business forward and being positioned to take the next step in your journey. Setting the right goals, choosing proven strategies, and developing a winning plan is what is needed to accomplish the goals necessary to grow your business. *The Masterpreneur Playbook*™ outlines the specific business goals for each step and lays out proven strategies for developing your winning plan.

A Goal Without A Plan Is A Wish

Let's take a quick look at the business goals you will have to accomplish at each step in the Masterpreneur Path™.

1) **Product Development** – good products and services provide a solution for a customer's need, want, or desire. There must also be sufficient potential market demand at a price point where you can make an appropriate profit margin.

2) **Market Acceptance** – finding the right target market, successfully reaching them, and meeting/exceeding their expectations so that your business can grow.

3) **Optimization** – continually analyzing and improving performance in all areas of your business.

4) **Planning for Growth** – developing new strategies for scaling and building the capacity necessary to satisfy increasing levels of demand. This includes people, inventory, equipment, and working capital.

5) **Implementation of Growth Plan** – putting your plans into action and actively managing performance to produce the best results possible.

Which of these business goals do you currently have?

- Is your primary business focused on developing the right products?
- Are you focused on determining who is most likely to buy your products and services?
- Do you focus most of your time on improving effectiveness and efficiency?

- Is your primary effort on developing a strategic growth plan for your business?
- Are you focused on implementing growth strategies and managing associated challenges?

What other business goals do you have?

- Increasing profitability?
- Succession planning?
- Growing Revenue?
- Financing?
- Others?

The Masterpreneur Evolution

You must also evolve as a business owner to complete each step of the Masterpreneur Path™ successfully. I call this process the Masterpreneur Evolution™, which outlines the roles and responsibilities you must embrace and master to successfully traverse the journey you will take from Starting-Up to Scaling your business. Since your business can go only as far as you can take it, you must continually learn and develop new skills to become a better manager and leader. *The Masterpreneur Playbook*™ outlines the specific personal and professional development stages that you will need to transform your organization at each step.

How Must Your Role Change as A Business Owner?

Let's take a quick look at the different roles you will have to play at each step of the Masterpreneur Path™.

1) **Entrepreneur** – exploring opportunities, evaluating opportunities, and developing a plan of action.

2) **Employee/Supervisor** – activities focused on the day-to-day or week-to-week

3) **Manager** – activities focused on continually improving business performance and results.

4) **Executive** – activities focused on strategic planning and future business growth opportunities.

5) **CEO** – activities focused on strengthening the brand externally and the internal culture of the business.

What is the primary role you play within your organization?

_____

- Are you still developing products and seeking to find the right market for them?
- Do you spend most of your time focused on the day-to-day or week to week?
- Do you spend most of your time focused on continually improving the business?
- Does your business run well independent of you so you can spend much of your time planning?
- Are you focused externally on building key relationships, accessing new markets, and understanding industry trends?

What other role(s) are you playing? _____

_____

- Entrepreneur?
- Employee?
- Supervisor?
- Manager?
- Executive?
- CEO?

Which role is the primary one you should be playing?

_____

- Entrepreneur?
- Employee?
- Supervisor?
- Manager?
- Executive?
- CEO?

Organizational Structure

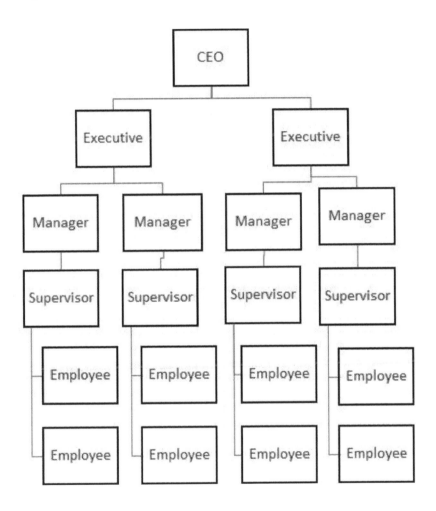

In the beginning, everyone does a little bit of everything. Since there are only a few people involved, everyone can easily be on the same page. The structure becomes more and more important the larger your organization grows because internal communication, clarity, and decision-making can become confusing or even dysfunctional. The goal should be to push tasks and decisions down to the lowest level possible in the company, but the opposite tends to happen in many businesses. Creating the right organizational structure at each step along the Masterpreneur Path™ is a balancing act that is extremely difficult for many business owners. As a result, very few small business owners ever develop a strong leadership team. Trying to grow without enough structure will cause you significant stress, work overload, and unnecessary headaches that you must deal with. *The Masterpreneur Playbook*™ will help you understand the delicate balance between structure and growth, outlining proven strategies for successful implementation.

Creating Order Out of The Chaos

Let's take a quick look at the organizational structure you will have to create at each step in the Masterpreneur Path™.

1) **No Employees** – most businesses are developed and start out with just the owner or owners.

2) **Employee(s)** – or independent contractors are needed to handle business growth and allow the business owner to focus on higher level more valuable tasks.

3) **Supervisor(s)** – you need a competent supervisor or supervisors to work on your business effectively. It is extremely difficult to manage continuous improvement while supervising the day-to-day operations.

4) **Manager(s)** – developing your leadership team by hiring competent managers with expertise and coaching them effectively results in continual improvement and frees you to focus on significantly growing your business.

5) **Executive(s)** – incorporating executive talent into your leadership team provides the administration and control functions necessary for

implementing and executing upon your growth strategies successfully.

What levels of organizational structure do you currently have?

_____

- Is it just you?
- Do you only have employees?
- Do you have one or more supervisors? If so, are they supervising the employees well?
- Do you have one or more managers? Are you micromanaging them?

Do you have an executive or an executive team? Are they driving the current and future growth and profitability of your company?

How much do you need? _____

- What level of structure can your organization support at this time?
- How much overhead can you handle given the scale of your business?
- Are you prepared to onboard and develop people into higher level roles?

Leadership Skills

    Being a successful business owner is all about leadership. There are several leadership styles and many different leadership skills to develop. However, there is a most critical leadership skill for achieving success in each of the 5-steps along the Masterpreneur Path™. Fortunately, leadership skills can be learned and developed rather than something you are born with. There are many leadership and management skills to be developed and honed during your journey. Your ability to master the right ones at the correct times will make or break your ability to successfully implement the *Masterpreneur Playbook*'s proven strategies to move your business forward along the Masterpreneur Path™.

It All Starts with The Person in The Mirror

Let's take a quick look at the leadership skills you will have to develop at each step in the Masterpreneur Path™.

1) Problem Solving

2) Communication

3) Analyzing Information

4) Coaching Managers

5) Inspiring Key Stakeholders

Which of these leadership skills do you need to develop?

- Are you a good problem solver?
- Do you communicate clearly and concisely?
- How well do you analyze quantitative and qualitative information to make informed decisions?
- What is your capacity for coaching others to achieve better results by asking them key questions?

What other leadership skills do you need to develop?

- Listening?
- Decisiveness?
- Dependability?
- Trust/Integrity?
- Influence?
- Self-Awareness?
- Creativity?

What is your leadership style? (Choose from styles below)

- Autocratic - The most illustrative phrase is, "Do as I say."
- Authoritative Style - Most indicative phrase "Follow me"
- Pacesetting Style - "Do as I do!" is most indicative phrase.
- Democratic Style - More likely to ask, "What do you think?"
- Coaching Style - Tend to have a "Consider this" approach."
- Affiliative Style - Often described by "People come first."
- Laissez-Faire Style - The opposite of the autocratic style.

Which leadership style do you employ most often?

_____

- Autocratic - "Do as I say."
- Authoritative Style - "Follow me"
- Pacesetting Style - "Do as I do!"
- Democratic Style - "What do you think?"

- Coaching Style - "Consider this" approach."
- Affiliative Style - "People come first."
- Laissez-Faire Style – "Do what you think is best."

Which leadership style is most unlike you?

_____

- Autocratic - "Do as I say."
- Authoritative Style - "Follow me"
- Pacesetting Style - "Do as I do!"
- Democratic Style - "What do you think?"
- Coaching Style - "Consider this" approach."
- Affiliative Style - "People come first."
- Laissez-Faire Style – "Do what you think is best."

How well are you able to "Flex" ~~between~~ among leadership styles depending on whom you interact with?

_____

- Can you easily communicate with people in a style that they will respond to well?
- Or are you a "one trick pony" treating everyone the same such that you connect well with some people and rub many others the wrong way?

Walking The Path

The Masterpreneur Playbook clearly lays out the path that your business must traverse and the evolution you must ~~experience~~ undertake to continually move your business forward and grow. Making good business decisions is the key to staying on the path, especially since your business can only go as far as you are prepared to take it. The key to making good business decisions is basing them on current, accurate information that is both quantitative and qualitative. The only way to do this is through creating processes and procedures for every aspect of your business.

The Small Business Pro (SBPro) Methodology introduced in my first book, *Running Your Small Business Like A Pro* outlines a three-step strategic planning process that will help you to obtain and process the necessary information to make the best possible decisions and implement the associated strategies effectively for growing your business. The 3-Steps are...

Step 1: Assessment & Visualization - obtain an objective determination of where things currently stand and develop a clear picture of where you want to be.

Step 2: Analysis & Recommendations - involves examining the information obtained from Step 1, studying the environment, and exploring options to determine the best course of action.

Step 3: Implementation & Evaluation - putting your plans into action and measuring performance against metrics so that you can make regular adjustments to better achieve the results that you desire.

This book is focused on Step 1: Assessment & Visualization since we help you to better understand where you are and lays out a clear path for moving your business forward successfully. From there you can better analyze your situation and determine where you are and what you should do next.

SBPro® Methodology

Use the table on the following page to do a preliminary assessment of your business and you. Circle the words in the boxes with statements that best represent your status.

Step	1	2	3	4	5
Path	ON the Concept	IN the Business	ON the Business	ON the Future	ON Scaling
Business Goals	Product and Services	Market Acceptance	Processes and Procedures	Strategic Growth Plan	Rapid Growth
Key Challenges	Marketing Plan	Target Market	Ability To Manage	Leadership Team	Growth and Cash Flow
Evolution	Entrepreneur	Employee / Supervisor	Manager	Executive	CEO
Structure	Usually, No Employees	Maybe Employees	Supervisor(s)	Manager(s)	Executive(s)
Leadership Skills	Problem Solving	Communicating	Analysis	Coaching	Inspiring

Now that you have a better understanding of where you are, it is important to envision where you are going. Please answer the questions below to identify some of your goals for the future...

Growth Goals

Your annual revenue goal needs to be at least $100k if you have not yet passed that threshold. Also, your revenue goals should be increasing year over year because "if you're not growing, you're dying." Your annual revenue goals should be at least 10%. The smaller your organization the higher your percentage revenue goal increase should be. Keep in mind that these are goals you should plan to achieve.

- Revenue Goal $_____

  o How much do you want your revenues to be next year? In 3 years? In 5 years?

As a business owner you'll generally work harder and make less money than if you had a job. This generally results from a combination of factors including not selling enough, not charging enough, and not managing expenses well enough. Your business should be able to pay you a salary (or draw) at least equal to the market rate for what your role and responsibilities are (i.e. how much you'd need to pay someone to perform your role.)

- Salary Goal $_____

   o   How much money do you want to make personally next year? In 3 years? In 5 years?

The goal of business is to make a profit (Sales – expenses = Profit or Loss). Just making enough to pay yourself a market rate salary is just breaking even. You need to make profit beyond that to have a sustainable business and fund future growth.

- Profitability Goal Beyond Salary $_____

   o   How profitable do you want your company to be next year? In 3 years? In 5 years?

You'll need to hire and/or contract with people to achieve your revenue, salary, and profit goals. Employees provide you with the operational leverage to continually grow and increase profitability. Of course, you only want to bring on employees if it will result in an increase in your profitability within a short period of time.

- Employee Goal #_____

   o   How many employees do you plan to have next year? In 3 years? In 5 years?

Location / Placement Goals

Continual growth requires increased capacity and often requires more space, even with virtual businesses. It is important to plan and budget for this growth a year in advance because it could easily take that long to find and fully transition to a new or additional location. You should most likely plan to own your location at some point in time to have a tangible asset that adds value to your business. It also helps you to manage expenses, avoid unnecessary disruptions, and have greater stability.

- # Physical Locations _____

  o How many physical locations do you plan to have next year? In 3 years? In 5 years?

- Facility Size _____ Square Feet
  o What size facilities do you plan to have next year? In 3 years? In 5 years?

- Own or Rent Facility _____

  o Do you plan to rent or own your facilities next year? In 3 years? In 5 years?

Succession Planning Goals

It is important to begin with the end in mind, per Stephen Covey. There are multiple succession planning options, and it will take at least 3 years of preparation to exit. Common exit types include selling to a partner, family member, key employee(s), competitor, supplier, customer, and investor(s) or just shutting the business down. Unfortunately, most businesses just shut down because of a combination of poor management and succession planning. You should also be working to create a sustainable business that can run without you because that will increase your options and maximize the value of your business. Unfortunately, many business owners fail to do this and end up with little or nothing to show for their years of hard work.

- Average Work Week _____ hours

    o How many hours do you want to work per week next year? In 3 years? In 5 years?

- Annual vacation days taken #_____

    o How many vacation days do you want to be able to take next year? In 3 years? In 5 years?

- Age When You Want to Exit _____

    o Do you want to exit the business next year? In 3 years? In 5 years?

- Type of Exit _____

    o If so, what type of exit do you want it to be next year? In 3 years? In 5 years?

- Business Value Upon Exiting _____

o   How much do you want your business to be worth upon exiting next year? In 3 years? In 5 years?

In the next chapters, we will explore each of the 5-Steps described in *The Masterpreneur™ Playbook* and review best practices for moving your business forward in the optimal way for achieving your goals. This will help you analyze the most appropriate information to recommend an optimal path to follow going forward.

STEP 1: Working ON the Concept of Your Business

When you are Working ON the Concept of Your Business, your job is to be entrepreneurial. Your task is to come up with ideas and figure out the best product and service offerings to deliver to potential customers. You also need to determine who is the correct target market that will place a high value on your offerings. Keep in mind that you are not really in business until you make the first sale.

The key challenge starting out, when you are Working ON the Concept of Your Business is developing a solid marketing plan which includes describing the business, defining the target market, understanding the competition, performing a SWOT analysis, setting goals, and creating a budget. Of course, there are many other things to do before diving into your business head-first, but none are more important to its overall success. The better a job you do with preparing before going into business, the more likely and the more rapidly you will have a viable business concept.

In step one, there are usually no full- time employees. It is just you and maybe a partner or assistant. You may also get help from friends and family when you can. Not surprisingly, there is little structure needed at this level. Think about the large companies like Microsoft® and HP® that were founded by people working out of their garage or basement.

"Defining Your Target Market"

Many companies go out of business quickly because either there is no viable market for their products, or the business owner is not able to find it in time (before running out of cash). Finding a sustainable market for your products is a critical step in the development of a successful business.

For Example, *The Masterpreneur Playbook* helped a client identify and accept the best target market for her products. Although she desired to sell to a different market, she met with very limited success and much frustration. The new target market immediately saw the value in her offering which made selling so much easier and enjoyable. Her feedback was, "Focusing my products on who is most likely to buy shifted my business trajectory in a great way."

Please complete the table below to identify the status of several important tasks you should complete during this step.

Checklist **Working ON the Concept of Your Business**			
Milestone	**Not Started**	**In Progress**	**Completed**
Select A Business Name			
Secure Domain Name and Set-Up Business Email			
Create An Entity			
Create/Update LinkedIn Profile			
Create Website			
Create/Update Other Social Media Profiles			
Get Industry Experience			
Narrowly Define Your Target Market			
Determine the amount of money you will need and where you plan to get it from			
Create financial projections and do A Breakeven Analysis			
Develop Monthly Sales Goals			
Setup Recordkeeping System			
Develop Relationships with Others In The Industry			
Check Out The Competition To See How You Compare			
Open A Business Bank Account			
Product Development			
Market Research			
Save Money			
Keep Track of Expenses			

STEP 2: Working IN Your Business

Opening your business and making sales denotes beginning the second step Working **IN** Your Business. At this stage, your role is more of an employee or supervisor who focuses on the day-to-day or week-to-week requirements of the business. This is where most business owners get stuck and never make it past stage two. Generally, less than 5% of all business owners ever rise above this level. So, what is the challenge? The challenge is that many business owners lack the necessary confidence or leadership skills and do not really know what they are supposed to do to move their organization forward. As a result, they remain stuck working in the business.

Do not get me wrong. There is nothing wrong with remaining at this level. It all depends on your goals and definition of success. I know many successful business owners who remain on Step 2 and are having a good life and making good money. The problem is they are generally tied to their business and unable to get away for a week without anxiety or experiencing a worrisome decrease in revenue. Many times, they must close for a period to get away. They must also work long hours and never seem to catch up with the workload. In addition, these types of businesses usually have minimal value and are not sellable, so eventually they just close when the owner is ready to leave. Think about working in your business for 10, 20, 30+ years and having to close the doors with nothing more to show for your efforts. Is that your goal? Do you want to be part of the five percent of businesses that successfully Level-Up to Step 3?

"Stuck at Second Base?"

At step two, you may or may not start with employees but will bring on more and more employees or contractors generally working alongside them. If your company continues to grow, you will need to play the role of a supervisor where you are still pretty much working alongside employees inside of the business. Less than 5% or 1 in 20 businesses successfully make it from Step 2 to Step 3.

For Example, *The Masterpreneur™ Playbook* helped a client who provided both text messaging and application development services which were really two businesses rather than one since they had different target markets. Focusing all of his marketing efforts on the text messaging services resulted in a sales increase and simplified his business. Client's feedback was "I was able to increase sales by 15% in just 3 months.

Please complete the table below to identify the status of several important tasks you should complete during this step.

Checklist **Working IN Your Business**			
Milestone	**Not Started**	**In Progress**	**Completed**
Business Networking Activities			
Implement Digital Marketing Strategy			
Develop Sales Skills			
Enhance And Adjust Product Offerings Based On Feedback From The Marketplace			
Develop a relationship with your banker			
Hire A Bookkeeper (internal or external)			
Register with SBDC and other non-profit organizations that provide free and discounted resources and services for entrepreneurs			
Access Business Counseling Services and get support from freelancers			

STEP 3: Working ON Your Business

As a business owner, to significantly move your business forward you must begin by Working ON Your Business. What does that mean? It means you have a longer-range perspective. You continuously work on improvement to optimize processes, create structure, and build the capacity necessary for sustainable growth. In Step 3 you will transition from being a technician to being a manager which requires different skills. Keep in mind that you cannot improve anything without measuring it. At this level you must employ professional management techniques and know the numbers of your business, which is a challenge for owners with limited business knowledge. You must go from owning a business to running your business!

Creating the structure necessary for you to elevate to step 3, the managerial role, can be extremely challenging. First, you will need to have a competent supervisor so that you can focus on managing. You must trust and empower supervisors which requires change. You will also have to delegate and get things done through others which may feel unnatural for both you and your employees, but necessary for growth. To complicate matters, you may not have anyone on the team with the capacity to supervise and you will have to hire from the outside which has its own challenges. Needless to say, many business owners get stuck here and cannot make this transition without help.

"Seek Help if You Want to Grow"

It is difficult to go from Working ON Your Business to Working ON the Future of Your Business. Less than 5% of businesses that successfully make it to Step 3 ever make it to step 4. Are you going to be that one business out of four hundred? I am sure that you want to but it is not enough to want it. You must be totally committed and willing to do whatever it takes however long it takes to get there. If this, is you, *The Masterpreneur Playbook*™ has the strategies that you want to follow to successfully make the transition.

For Example, *The Masterpreneur*™ *Playbook* helped a client to go from working in her business to working on her business. She learned to analyze her financials, identifying opportunities to improve cash flow, and run her business more effectively. She also put together a financing package that got her access to capital. In addition, she developed a strategic plan that got her team fired up and led to her business growing. Her testimonial is "I had my first strategic planning meeting with my staff yesterday. I rolled out the plan that Andrew and I had developed. They were fired up. I was fired up! It was like it's not just me with the mission, there's all these people, we're all on the same page --let's go! you know so I felt good about that."

Please complete the table below to identify the status of several important tasks you should complete during this step.

Checklist **Working ON Your Business**			
Milestone	**Not Started**	**In Progress**	**Completed**
Document And Upgrade Procedures			
Create Job Descriptions for Everyone			
Hire Accountant (internal or external)			
Create 3-Year Financial Projection			
Hire or Promote a Supervisor Position			
Establish Key Performance Indicators (KPI's) and review performance towards them weekly			
Review Financials Monthly and compare against the budget			
Standardize Processes and Develop Systems			
Find Ways To Increase Capacity			
Work On The Business Model			
Re-evaluate Branding and Messaging			
Hire a Business Coach			

STEP 4: Working ON the Future of Your Business

When you reach step four, you are Working ON the Future of Your Business with a focus on your business goal of strategic planning and preparing for rapid growth. You will effectively be creating a new business plan to totally re-invent your business and make it scalable. It is exceedingly difficult to create a viable plan for scaling if you have not yet optimized your business and built capacity while Working ON Your Business in step 3. Plus, you will need detailed marketing research and a strategic planning process which are much more effective when done with external assistance.

As a business owner you must be able to spend most of your time expanding your perspective, exploring new ideas, learning about the industry, and building relationships. That is why developing a strong leadership team is the Key Challenge during this step. You will never have the time and perspective to plan effectively if you are still trying to manage the business. As a result, you will need to backfill the manager role, develop the capacity to grow by being a leader of managers rather than continuing to try and manage everything yourself. Just hiring a manager is not enough, you must choose the right person and create the right onboarding program to ensure their success. This is much easier said than done and usually takes multiple hires and executive coaching to break your unproductive habits that may work well for managers, but not executives. That is why coaching is the most important leadership skill to develop during this step.

"You, As A Leader of Managers – No More Managing!"

And that's step four Working ON the Future Your Business. Even still, not many business owners successfully emerge from Working ON the Future of Your Business to Working ON Scaling Your Business. Similarly, less than 5% of businesses that successfully make it to Step 4 ever transition to Step 5. That means that only 1 out of 8,000 businesses ever make Step 5. What does it take to become one of them? Getting the help, you need by following *The Masterpreneur Playbook*™ of course.

For Example, *The Masterpreneur™ Playbook* helped a client to go from working on his business to working on the future of his business. He was able to restructure his organization, implement new processes and procedures, and create a strong leadership team giving him the bandwidth to focus on planning for future growth opportunities. His feedback was, "I gotta say that I'm glad that I trusted you with your plan because I like the plan, but it is a journey, but we're getting there and we're making real solid progress."

Please complete the table below to identify the status of several important tasks you should complete during this step.

Checklist **Working ON The Future of Your Business**			
Milestone	**Not Started**	**In Progress**	**Completed**
Hire or Promote Into A Manager Role			
Develop A Capital Budget			
Develop A Strategic Plan			
Consider New Product/ Service Offerings			
Update Mission, Vision, and Values			
Explore Opportunities for Market Expansion			
Prepare For Financing			
Hire a CPA (internal or external)			
Hire Business Consultant and Create an Advisory Board			

STEP 5: *Working ON Scaling Your Business*

Working ON Scaling Your Business is contingent on being able to successfully implement the plans and strategies developed while Working ON the Future of Your Business. Scaling a business is complex and requires you to be a symbol for others to focus on for both direction and inspiration. Here are some of the strategies that may need to be executed to scale successfully:

- Obtaining financing early to support business growth plans

- Driving revenue by increasing sales and marketing efforts

- Increasing inventory levels and output capacity

- Expanding footprint and setting up additional locations

- Investing in new equipment and machinery

Sounds expensive? Consider how expensive it is to go out of business. That is why incorporating professional management practices to continually optimize your business, build capacity, and measure performance are so important when Working ON Your Business. Developing your leadership team with the right people in the right roles who can work together effectively is another critical success factor to address while Working ON the Future of Your Business. Keep in mind that any unresolved issues or incomplete accomplishments during the previous steps will come to light and be magnified when Working ON Scaling Your Business.

"Strategy is Important, But Not Sufficient"
– Terry Trayvick

For example, *The Masterpreneur™ Playbook* helped a client navigate the challenges of scaling their business. They gained an understanding of how and why growing business requires ongoing capital investment even though they are becoming more profitable. Although they were already experiencing significant cash flow issues, we they able to carefully manage their cash until they were able to secure financing. We also put in place weekly KPI meetings where they continue to manage cash flow, review business drivers, and discuss important topics. The client's feedback was "You saved our company by helping us understand that we would need to access significant amounts of cash to achieve our growth plans. With your guidance we successfully managed through a cash crunch and we able to access capital in difficult times."

Please complete the table below to identify the status of several important tasks you should complete during this step.

Checklist **Working ON Scaling Your Business**			
Milestone	**Not Started**	**In Progress**	**Completed**
Hire A CPA Firm			
Obtain Financing			
Closely Manage Cash Flow			
Hire or Promote into Executive Roles			
Build and strengthen external Relationships			

Congratulations!

Now you're a Masterpreneur!!!

Conclusion

Trying to skip a Step or move forward before you are ready only makes your journey that much more difficult. Business owners start out Working IN Their Businesses unless they purchased an ongoing concern, or their ownership interest is purely financial. Keep in mind that this is a marathon, not a sprint and it generally takes years, not months, to master each Step and Level-Up. Very few companies experience the rapid growth that the darlings of the tech world achieve. The time it takes for your company to Level-Up will vary based on external factors such as industry, competition, market trends, and the economy. It also depends on several key organizational factors including capital, customers, resources, products/services, employees, marketing plan/budget, sales team, and reputation. On the personal side, your relationships, personality, creativity, leadership skills, and ability to learn will drive the ability to Level-Up.

If you did not know, now you know, and knowing is half the battle because you cannot solve a problem if you don't understand the root cause. Just addressing the symptoms is not sustainable. *The Masterpreneur Playbook*™ outlines proven strategies for solving the key business challenges that you will face. At the end of the day, you may not like the solution, and you will have to do the work, but that is the price of success.

"SUCCESS Only Comes Before WORK in the Dictionary"

My goal is to empower YOU and 1,000 other business owners annually to be more likely to successfully transition from Working IN Your Businesses to Working ON Your Businesses. That is why I created *The Masterpreneur Playbook*™ and Founded the Small Business Pro University (www.SBProU.com). We meet you where you are on your business journey and guide you toward creating a sustainable enterprise that can successfully run without you. Of course, you will need help because nobody makes it alone. That is why we also offer expert coaching, consulting, and training services to prepare you, develop your team, and help you implement strategies outlined in *The Masterpreneur™ Playbook*.

Recommended Reading

5 Second Selling
by Paul Holland

10 Ways To Get Sued by Anyone and Everyone: The Small Business Owners Guide To Staying Out of Court
by Mitchell C. Beinhaker, Esq. and Barry H. Cohen

10 Ways to Screw Up an Ad Campaign
by Barry H. Cohen

A Setback Is A Set-Up for A Comeback
by Willie Jolley

Blue Ocean Strategies
by W. Chan Kim and Renée Mauborgne

Built to Sell
by John Warrillow

E-Myth Revisited & E-Myth Mastery
by Michael Gerber

Finish Big
by Bo Burlingham

How to Win Friends and Influence People
by Dale Carnegie

Lean Start-Up
by Eric Ries

Most Likely to Succeed: The Frazier Formula for Success
by Evan Frazier

My Business Plan Book
by Laurana Edwards

Strategic Influence

by Dale Caldwell

The 1-Page Marketing Plan
by Allan Dib

The 7 Habits of Highly Successful People
by Steven R. Covey

The Lonely Entrepreneur
by Michael Dermer

The Millionaire Next Door
by Michael Dermer

The Richest Man in Babylon
by George S. Clason

The Wealthy Barber
by David Chilton

Think and Grow Rich: A Black Choice
by Dennis Kimbro

Who Moved My Cheese?
by Spencer Johnson

Why Should White Guys Have All the Fun?
by Reginald Lewis

Andrew Frazier, MBA, CFA

Business Growth Pro and CFO
Founder, Small Business Pro University

Andrew Frazier empowers business owners to <u>Maximize the Value</u> of their companies by helping them Grow Revenue, Increase Profitability, and Obtain Financing. He guides them along the critical path to creating a sustainable business that can run without them through invaluable coaching, consulting, and training services. Mr. Frazier has worked 1-on-1 with 1,000+ business owners and taught thousands of people about business. His expertise in business strategy and financial management enables him to take a holistic perspective and provide more optimal solutions for clients.

Mr. Frazier's book "<u>Running Your Small Business Like A Pro</u>" helps people increase the likelihood and magnitude of their success in business. He has also produced <u>POWER BREAKFAST</u> events in Northern NJ for more than 10 years generating $10+ million in both economic impact and financing for 1,000+ attendees.

Recently he was recognized by US Senator Cory Booker and NJ Governor Phil Murphy for his contributions to the small business community. His online Small Business Pro University provides entrepreneurs with access to best practices and useful knowledge for running their businesses more professionally.

Andrew hosts the Leadership LIVE @ 8:05! – Talking Small Business podcast and livestreams. His articles have appeared in Professional Performance Magazine, Manufacturing Matters, the digital edition of Sales and Marketing Management, and "Octane", the worldwide Entrepreneurs' Organization's (EO) blog, Inc.com and "SmallbizDaily.com, "Americanentrepreneurship.com, and NJ Business magazine". He was also interviewed on RVN.TV Family Business World show and the syndicated "School for Startups Radio" show.

Andrew graduated from MIT with a BS in Mechanical Engineering, earned an MBA in Finance from NYU, and achieved the Chartered Financial Analyst (CFA) designation. His background includes significantly diverse experiences as a Naval Officer, Operations Manager, Corporate Executive, Investment Manager, Real Estate Investor, Non-Profit Leader, Board Member, Business Owner, Professor, Coach, Consultant, Trainer, and Author. Learn more about Andrew from his LinkedIn profile at https://www.linkedin.com/in/andrewfrazier.

Mr. Frazier has been married for 30+ years, has two children, and lives in Montclair, NJ.

www.SmallBusinessLikeAPro.com

www.SBProU.com

Additional Websites

- **Livestream and Podcast** – www.LiveAt805.com
- **Blog -** https://www.sbprou.com/sbpro-blog

Social Media

LinkedIn
- Personal Profile: AndrewFrazier
  - https://www.linkedin.com/in/andrewfrazier/
- Company Page:
  - https://www.linkedin.com/company/small-business-pro-university

Facebook
- Personal Profile: Andrew.Frazier.Jr
  - https://www.facebook.com/andrew.frazier.jr/
- Company Page: SBProU
  - https://www.facebook.com/SBProU/

Twitter
- @Andrew_Frazier
  - https://twitter.com/Andrew_Frazier
- @SmBizLikeAPro
  - https://twitter.com/SmBizLikeAPro

Instagram
- Small_Business_Like_A_Pro
  - https://www.instagram.com/andrew_frazier_sbpro/

YouTube
- Small Business Pro University
  - https://www.youtube.com/c/SmallBusinessProUniversity

Helping entrepreneurs & small businesses owners to…

Grow Revenues
Increase Profitability
Obtain Financing

Providing entrepreneurs, business owners, and organizational leaders with access to the expertise, tools, and resources they need to compete effectively in this fast paced, technology driven, global business environment. Our services include:

- Coaching
- Consulting
- Training
- Speaking

www.RunningYourSmallBusinessLikeAPro.com

Small Business Pro University (SBProU)

Mission

Help 1,000,008 Entrepreneurs and Businesses Owners Grow Revenues, Increase Profitability, and Obtain Financing by 2028.

Vision

Become the leader at providing entrepreneurs, small business owners, and organizational leaders with access to the expertise, tools, and resources they need to compete effectively in this fast-paced, technology-driven, global business environment.

Values

Using Creativity to effectively combine Knowledge with Experience for entrepreneurs and small business owners to achieve Continual Improvement throughout their journey to develop a sustainable enterprise.

www.SBProU.com

SBProU Offerings

Courses
- Individual Courses
- Bundled Courses

Training Programs
- Masterpreneur Training Program
- Masterpreneur Growth Accelerator

Coaching Programs
- 1-on-1
- SBPro Strategic
- Masterpreneur Playbook

SBPro University Press
- Books and Workbooks

Membership Groups
- Small Business Pro Network
- The Masterpreneur Club

Leadership LIVE @ 8:05 – Talking Small Business
- Livestream – Tuesdays @ 8pm EST
- Podcast – Thursdays @ 8am EST

SBProU Press

The current books published by the Small Business Pro University Press are as follows...

- Running Your Small Business Like A Pro
- Running Your Small Business Like A Pro – WORKBOOK
- The Masterpreneur Playbook

The Small Business Pro University Press is continually expanding its library of valuable business books for entrepreneurs. The following books are some of the books currently under development...

- Get Your Business Financed Faster and Easier
- Secrets To Maximizing Profitability
- How To Sell More with Customer-Centric Marketing
- Market Your Business Like a Drug Dealer and Win More Customers

Since everybody learns in their own way, SBPro University Press be making these books available in several formats including...

- Paperback (English and Spanish)
- eBook
- Audiobook
- Multimedia Book
- Courses (In-Person, Virtual, and Online)

25% Off

The Masterpreneur Training Programs

https://www.sbprou.com/special-offer

Thank you for purchasing my book.

Andrew Frazier, MBA, CFA
Founder, Small Business Pro University
Andrew@MySBPro.com
www.SBProU.com

Made in the USA
Middletown, DE
13 December 2023

44524256R00046